Don't Say the Words

by Tom Holloway

Currency Press,
Sydney

GRIFFIN
THEATRE COMPANY

Principal Sponsor
PKF
Chartered Accountants
& Business Advisers

CURRENCY PLAYS

First published in 2008
by Currency Press Pty Ltd,
PO Box 2287, Strawberry Hills, NSW, 2012, Australia
enquiries@currency.com.au
www.currency.com.au
in association with
Griffin Theatre Company, Sydney

NATIONAL LIBRARY OF AUSTRALIA CIP DATA

Author:	Holloway, Tom.
Title:	Don't say the words / author, Tom Holloway.
ISBN:	9780868198347 (pbk.)
Series:	Current theatre series.
Subjects:	Australian drama–21st century.
Dewey Number:	A822.4

Typeset by Dean Nottle for Currency Press.
Cover photograph by Olivia Martin-McGuire.

Currency Press acknowledges the Traditional Owners of the Country on which
we live and work. We pay our respects to all Aboriginal and Torres Strait
Islander Elders, past and present.

Don't Say the Words was first performed by Griffin Theatre Company and the Tasmanian Theatre Company at the SBW Stables Theatre, Sydney, on 2 July 2008, with the following cast:

A	Jack Finsterer
C	Anna Lise Phillips
AE	Brett Stiller

Director, Matthew Lutton
Dramaturg, Peter Matheson
Designer, Adam Gardnir
Lighting Designer, Paul Jackson
Composer / Sound Designer, Kelly Ryall

CHARACTERS

A, a man
C, a woman
AE, a man

Don't Say the Words was inspired by the play
Agamemnon by Aeschylus.

SCENE ONE

We see A. *He sings the first two choruses and verses of 'History Never Repeats', by the Split Enz. He is cut off halfway through the first line of the third chorus.*

SCENE TWO

We see C *and* A.

C: He ah…

A: Yes?

C: He held my hair back.

A: Yes…

C: Pulled it. He pulled my hair back with his hand.

A: No.

C: What?

A: How?

C: How? With his—

A: Yes his hand or his—

C: Sorry, I don't—

A: Or his—

C: I don't—

A: With his hand, yes, or his fist?

      A *demonstrates.*

C: Oh.

A: Yes?

C: He held my hair back with his fist.

A: Okay.

C: He ripped. He ripped my hair back with his fist.

A: Ripped. Good. He ripped your hair back with his fist. And?

C: He said—

A: Said?

C: Yes.

A: Not shouted?

C: No.

A: He wasn't. You know. In a rage? In some kind of fiery rage?

C: No. Not yet. He ripped my hair back. Yes. Ripped it. But like a warning or a statement or something. He wasn't yet in a fiery rage. Not yet.

A: Okay. And?

C: He talked about the barbeque.

A: The one—

C: The one we had just had.

A: When he got home?

C: Yes.

A: The family barbeque to celebrate him arriving—

C: Yes.

A: Arriving home?

C: Yes. Arriving home.

A: To celebrate?

C: Yes. To—

A: And what did he say?

C: Why?

A: Because—

C: No. Why. He said why. Asked. He ripped my hair back with his fist like as a warning, quite casual. Slow. Like it could almost have been intimate if it wasn't a fist and if he didn't rip quite so hard. And he asked why did I ask him to sit at the head of the table.

A: And did you ask him to sit at the head of the table?

C: Yes I did. Of course. It's his family. His barbeque. His table. He had returned home after a long time. A long time off fighting at—

A: Yes.

C: And this was his family and his barbeque and his place was at the head of the—

A: But…

C: He said no. He wouldn't. He refused.

A: Why?

C: He said it wasn't his place.

A: Why wasn't it his place?

C: I don't know.

A: Not 'I don't know'.

C: But—

A: Had someone else been sitting there, while he was away? Fighting. Fighting for. At the very front line of. Had someone else been sitting at the head of the table?

C: No.

A: Had there been someone else sitting there?

C: No!

A: Come on.

C: Yes.

A: So he ripped your hair back with his fist and he asked you casually why, why had you asked him to sit at the head of the table of his family when he knew someone else had been sitting there while he was fighting at the very front line of hell. Right. Okay. Is that about right?

C:

A: Then what did he do?

C: Shouted.

A: Now he shouted?

C: Yes.

A: So now he's in a fiery rage?

C: He's building. He's begun to build to it. Yes.

A: Good.

C: He put his other hand. Sorry. Fist. In front of my face and. Sorry. No.

A: It's okay.

C: He ripped my hair back with his fist and put his other fist. His tattooed fist in front of my face and shouted at me to—

A: Did he shout?

C: Sorry?

A: It's just… I know I said before, but did he actually maybe whisper? Did he shout or did he maybe whisper?

C: Whisper?

A: Yes.

C: No.

A: You know how. Did he whisper? Up close. Did he rip your hair back with his fist and then put. No. Shove. Shove his other fist. His tattooed fist. Good. That's good. In your face and then whisper? Whisper up close to you—

C: No I don't—

A: Because you know how people can. People like him can. Violent people. And we're not. I'm pretty sure we're not disputing that he isn't violent, are we?

C: No.

A: I mean he fights. He fights in bloody wars so…

C: Yes.

A: Well, you know how people like him. Violent people like him even when in a fiery rage. Can seem calm? You know? Real calm?

C: No. But. I know. I know how people like him. Violent people like him can be calm. But he. If we're going to. Then he shouted. He spat in my face as he shouted.

A: Okay.

C: He shouted real loud and spat in my face as he shouted look at my fucking—

A: He swore? Are you sure he? Because. You know. Isn't that a little obvious?

C: What?

A: Swearing like that. Isn't that a little bit too obvious?

C: Fuck you.

A: Okay.

C: Obvious? I mean fucking—

A: Okay.

C: He screamed at me. He spat in my face as he screamed at me look at my fucking hand! What does it say on my fucking hand?! I mean now. Now he is well and truly raging. And he screamed at me what does it say on my fucking—

A: Good. And you know?

C: What it—

A: You know what it said?

C: Of course I fucking—

A: Because. You know. It sounds important to him. That sounds like it's pretty bloody important to him.

C: Of course I—

A: I mean he comes back. Comes back from the very front line of hell. From his tour to the worst. The most awful battle he has ever been in. All over. He writes you letters telling you he seems to be fighting. Well for nothing. All over nothing and that you are all that keeps him going. And he comes back with that on his hand. Like the only thing he has been thinking about that whole time was you. I reckon that sounds like it's an important thing for you to—

C: My name. It said my name. One letter on each finger. My fucking name. Do I know? Do I? Yes. Fucking yes. Yes I know. Okay? He pulled. He ripped my hair back with his fist. He shoved. Shoved his other fist. His tattooed fist in my face. He shouted at me. Screamed at me and spat in my face as he screamed at me to look at his fucking fist. To read what it said on his fucking fist that he has been doing god knows what with on the, I mean you said it, on the very front line of hell, and what is said was. What it fucking said was. Each letter tattooed. Badly. Over a fire or something. So it looks really bad. Really crap. Each letter on a different fucking finger looking really fucking crap, was my name. My fucking. So don't. Don't you…

A:

C: Do I know!

A: Jesus.

C: Yes, jesus. Fucking hell.

A: What. Sorry but. What then?

C:

A: What then?

C: He hit me.

A: Hit you?

C: Yes.

A: Hit you where?

C: On the nose.

A: Sorry?

C: On the—

A: He hit you on the nose?

C: Yes.

A: No that's not. Sorry but that's not right.

C: Sorry?

A: He hit you on the nose?

C: Yes! Yes! He hit me on the fucking—

A: But that sounds.

C: Nose! Sounds what?

A: I don't know but that sounds. I mean he ripped your hair back with his fist. He shoved his other fist. His tattooed fist in your face and shouted at you. Screamed at you and spat in your face as he screamed at you to read what was on his fucking. And on each finger. On each fucking finger was a different letter of your name. Your fucking name. No matter what it looked like. And then he. Then he just hit you on the nose? Sorry but no. That sounds. Well, it just sounds too—

C: Look. He fucking punched me in the fucking face and broke my. I think he might have broken my fucking nose!

A: Good!

C: Okay?

A: Good! That's good! Better than hit you on the nose. He punched you in the fucking face and broke your. You think he might have broken your fucking nose. Good. Did it hurt?

C: You arsehole.

A: Did it?

C: Yes.

A: Good. And?

C:

A: And?

C: Good?

A:

C: He threw me into the fridge.

A: Like pushed? Pushed you hard?

C: Yes pushed me hard in to the fridge then threw me onto the table but it. I think he picked me up and threw me onto the table but it broke.

A: When you—

C: It broke under me and I fell on to the ground. The tiles. The kitchen, ah. Has tiles and. The back of my head hit against the tiles on the. And

I'm bleeding. My nose is bleeding. My lip is bleeding. The back of my head is bleeding. And he jumps on me and.

A: Oh jesus. Oh baby.

C: Don't call me that.

A: Oh jesus. I want to. I just want to—

C: Yells at me. Screams at me I'm a bitch. A cheating bitch slut and a bitch and there's no way he can put up with that. Look at my hand he says. Look at my hand. I do that for you and you go and. With my best. You're a bitch. A fucking cheating bitch and you're going to get a hiding like you fucking. I can't put up with that so I'm sorry. I'm so sorry baby but. He said this. Sorry. I'm so sorry but I'm going to have to beat the hell out of you.

A: So he pushes you hard against the fridge. Then he picks you up. Picks you up and throws you onto the table. The table breaks. You fall to the. The back of your head hits the tiled floor and you're bleeding and he jumps on you and. And he calls you a. Screams out that you. That you're a—

C: Well I mean I am.

A: What?

C: I am.

A: Are what?

C: I am cheating on him.

A: Sorry?

C: I am.

A: So?

C: I'm just saying I am. I mean I'm not saying. Not trying to say that what he's doing is… is okay, but… But I mean I'm not. We're not—

A: Are you joking?

C: We're not totally innocent. Me and my lover. We're not.

A: I mean are you joking? Shut up! Shut up with that. That's bullshit. That's totally—

C: And it's not just some fling. It's love, isn't it? I'm in love with my lover, which is the worst kind of cheating because it means I'm not in love with him. And is that all that surprising considering the things he has done to me? To our family? The things he has made me do? Made me give up? Bundling me out of town and sending me off to the city to 'clear up a mistake' as he goes off to war? I mean did he ever think that he might be the reason why someone else has been sitting at the head of the fucking—

A: Shut up with that stuff! We can't. There's no place for opening up things like that here, okay? We gotta get this. If we don't get this right then. Then this just isn't going to… So just… Okay? Okay?

C:

A: So he yells at you and then what?

C: He hits me again.

A: Right.

C: Punches me.

A: Good.

C: Knocks my head against the tiled floor.

A: Right. Good.

C: Picks it up and knocks it hard against. Punches me and smashes my head hard against the—

A: Good. Smashes. Good.

C: Over and over. With one hand he's smashing my head. Smashing it into the ground. And with the other hand. Other fist. He's punching me and that's the tattooed fist.

A: Yes.

C: He's punching me with the tattooed fist and smashing my head with the other.

A: And?

C: I'm lying there.

A: Right.

C: In the kitchen.

A: Right.

C: On the ground in the kitchen.

A: Yes.

C: And as he beats me—

A: Yes.

C: As he beats me the only thing I can think of—

A: Right.

C: Is my name on his tattooed fist.

A: Good!

C: Over and over. That fist. My name.

A: The tattoo. Right!

C: Until my eyes swell up and all I feel are these—

A: Yes?

C: Thuds.

A: Good!

C: These distant thuds and even then.

A: Right. Yes?

C: Still even then when I can't see.

A: Yes?

C: When my eyes are.

A: Yes?

C: With the thuds going on. Over and over.

A: Of course.

C: Even then he is screaming at me about it. About what he did. About what it means for him to wear that forever and the only thing I can see in my mind is that tattoo and that fist.

A: Good.

C: And then…

A: Good baby.

C: Then…

A: Good…

C: Then it stops.

A: Stops?

C: Yes. Stops.

A: Just like—

C: That's how you'd like it, isn't it? That as he's hitting me like a bull. Like a raging bull. That I'm not thinking of my lover. That I'm not thinking I wish he had died. Been killed brutally. Blown to a thousand parts while at war so I could sleep warm and safe in my lover's arms. I'm not thinking how that would have fixed all of this. That I'm not thinking about that but in fact thinking about that crappy tattoo that he has come back with.

A:

C: That's what you would like, isn't it?

A: How can you? But how can you tell that it's stopped? After a beating like that? How are you with-it enough to know that? Are you not out cold? Has he not beaten you so badly that you have shut down and you are out cold?

C:

A:

C: I don't know. Perhaps. But something brings me back. He gets off me. The thuds stop and I am brought back when I feel him. It feels all distant but I feel him get off me.

A: Get off your chest?

C: Yes.

A: And?

C: I feel him get off me. Off my chest. Off my breasts—

A: Your breasts?

C: Yes my breasts that he sits on as he punches and smashes me but that my lover falls asleep against gently. That—

A: And?

C: He runs a bath for himself. He leaves me there on the floor and he goes and runs a bath and gets in.

A: He gets off. Sorry. He gets off your breasts after. After all. He punches you and beats your. I'm sorry. But beats your head hard against the tiled floor and he does all this over and over. And then he runs himself a bath?

C: And sits down in it and has a cigarette.

A: Are you. Are you sure?

C: I hear him sit in the water and light a cigarette.

A: You're sure?

C: Yes I'm sure.

A: But I mean. How?

C: He always has a bath when he comes home and when he has one he always has a cigarette. I know those sounds. When you live with someone. When you. You get to know things just by sounds. By little. And I know those sounds. The creak of the taps. The running water. The particular splash of the water that his body makes when he gets in the bath. The click of his gas lighter. His first inhale. I know them. When he is away. When he is not here I find myself imagining them even. Like ghosts.

A: Okay. So he does that. Does all that and then. Then just goes and sits down in the bath and has a fucking cigarette. Right. Okay. Sure. If you. And what? What do you do?

C: I get up.

A: After all that?

C: I get up slowly. I sit up. It is very difficult. The pain. The dizziness. I pull myself to my feet. I feel like I'm drunk. I'm weak on my feet. Swaying. My head feels all. I grab a cloth. A tea towel and wipe my face. It helps me see again.

A: Is there blood? Is there a lot of—

C: Oh yes. The tea towel is wet. My clothes are wet. Yes there is a lot of—

A: Then what?

C: I walk. I walk real slow. I'm shaking. My hands are shaking and I walk real slow in to the bedroom.

A: To lie down?

C: No. Not to lie down. I walk real slow in to the bedroom and get his gun. His 303.

A: Sorry?

C: I get his 303.

A: His gun?

C: That he uses when he goes roo shooting.

A: You choose. You decide to go and get his gun?

C: Yes. Well, no. But. I am scared. Scared he might start again. I am barely—

A: Yes…

C: Barely aware of what I am doing.

A: Good. You are barely aware of what you are doing. Good. So you know where he keeps it, his gun?

C: Of course I do. In the bedroom. He has a cabinet. Dark wood and felt interior. Like he cares more about his guns than—

A: And you know how to shoot it?

C: He taught me. Got me shooting jars and old cans and stuff in the paddock. Out the back in the—

A: And you get it? You go and get it while he sits in the bath?

C: I get the 303 and it's loaded. He always keeps it loaded. Like some threat. And then I—

A: And him? What is he doing all this—

C: He's still sitting in the bath.

A: Still?

C: Just sitting there.

A: The whole time?

C: Yes. I can hear the slight flap of water against porcelain. He thinks I'm out cold.

A: Right. Okay. I see.

C: So I walk back in to the kitchen and…

A: We're almost there baby.

C: And…

A: Step over the…

C: Step over the broken table.

A: With blood all…

C: And there's blood all everywhere and I…

A: I'm shaking.

C: I'm shaking and I walk to the bathroom and—

A: The door's open to the bathroom.

C: The door's open to the bathroom and I walk up to him and he turns and looks at me standing there all beaten. The gun in his face. Pointing right in his face and he looks. For a second. Looks surprised and then I…

A: Yes…

C: I get a flash of everything he has done. All the good things. All the bad.

A: Right.

C: I get a flash of it all and I get this wave. This wave of rage and of… of… And then I shoot him. I shoot him in the. In the fucking head. Shoot him. Three times. I stand there standing over him and when he looks at me. Surprised. Well, I don't know. It. It kind of shocks me and I feel all those things and before I know what I've done. Before I can think I pull the trigger three times and I shoot him in the head. Just like. Just like that. Just shoot him like that.

A: Good.

C: I shoot him right there in the. Because I. I just. I can't take it anymore and. All this. All the. So I get up off the ground. I get his gun and I shoot him in the fucking head right there in the bath because I just can't. Can't stand it anymore and…

A: Good. Right. Well done.

C:

A: But baby. But. What then? What did you do then?

C: What?

A: What did you do then?

C: What? What did I? I called the. Called the police. I shot him dead and then called the police.

A: Good.

C:

A: Baby.

C:

A: This is good baby. This is right.

C:

A: This is right baby.

C: Don't call me that.

A: But.

C: Don't call me baby. I'm not your baby.

A: Okay. Okay I… Okay.

C:

A: Thank you.

C: Don't you say that. Don't you dare—

A: Okay.

C: God.

A: Well I. I better get ready. Better go and get—

C: I will do this.

A: Just beers with a mate. Maybe a bit of The Ashes on the big screen. Maybe the same karaoke. They still got that machine there?

C: I said—

A: Yeah. I hope so. I feel like a bit of a sing.

C: Did you —

A: But you know, don't wait up yeah?

C: Are you listening? I will fucking do this.

A: What?

C: Are you fucking listening to what I am fucking saying?

A: Yeah right. Okay.

C: Are you fucking listening?

A: Won't be late. Okay.

> A *leaves.*

C: Yes. Well. Hurry back.

SCENE THREE

We see the back of AE. *He stands at a urinal, pissing. He whistles the beginning of 'He Ain't Heavy' by The Hollies to himself. He then mumbles through the words of the first verse, not really remembering the lyrics all that well.*

As he gets into the first chorus he gets a bit more into the song, starting to sing louder, but still getting words wrong.

Without putting his penis away, he takes out a black texta or pen while he sings the next verse, still getting words wrong. As he sings he writes on the wall… 'He ain't heavy, he's my—'

He stops writing and singing. He stares at the wall. He uses his sleeve to rub the words out. They smudge but don't quite disappear. He then writes over the top… 'FUCK YOU ARSE FUCKER'.

He takes a moment, puts his penis away, does up his fly and then leaves.

SCENE FOUR

We see A *and* AE.

A & AE: [*together*] Our lager,

    Which art in barrels,

    Hallowed be thy drink,

    Thy will be drunk,

    (I will be drunk)

    At home as I am in the tavern.

    Give us this day our foamy head,

    And forgive us our spillages,

    As we forgive those who spill against us,

    And lead us not to incarceration,

    But deliver us from hangovers,

    For thine is the beer,

    The bitter and the lager,

    Forever and ever,

    Barmen.

    Up ya arse and scull the glass!

A: Cheers.

AE: Cheers mate.

A / AE:

AE: So. The warrior. The bloody hero warrior cousin finally returns from the bloody god-awful war that everyone thought would never end. How about that, hey? How about bloody that?

A: Sure.

AE: You know I've been sittin' here lookin' at these TVs each time it came up on the news thinkin', is that me cuz up there?

A: Right.

AE: Is that me bloody cousin up there bein' a big fuckin' hero?

A: Sure.

AE: But it wasn't, was it? Not you. Your kind of work doesn't get shown on the news now, does it? That's what I've heard.

A: That's what you've heard, is it mate?

AE: That's what I've bloody heard.

A: Right.

AE: Yeah, right. I've heard the kind of shit you do isn't really appropriate for a news headlines. Isn't that right mate? SAS, right? Isn't that right?

A:

AE: Well. Good to have ya back, me mate. Cheers to that, hey?

A: Yeah. Cheers to that.

AE / A:

A: What's the? What's going—

AE: Huh?

A: Has it—

AE: Started?

A: Yeah.

AE: Nah mate.

A: Nah?

AE: Still, ya know—

A: Huh?

AE: Still rainin'.

A: Really?

AE: Yeah.

A: Shit.

AE:

A: Bloody. You know. Bloody England.

AE: Huh?

A: Bloody—

AE: Yeah.

A: Always bloody—

AE: Yeah. Cheers to—

A: Always bloody raining in bloody England.

AE: Cheers to that mate. Cheers to bloody—

A: Yeah.

AE: Up y'arse.

A: Yeah.

AE:

A: You know. Hold on. Ah, beers over there…

AE: Yeah?

A: Beers. Yeah. Are flat. Real stodgy too. Stodgy and flat and—

AE: Yeah?

A: Yeah and weak.

AE: Weak?

A: Yeah. You know. Like. What was it? Three percent most of 'em.

AE: Three percent?

A: Yeah.

AE: Jesus. Three percent?

A: Bloody hell.

AE: Why? You know—

A: Bother?

AE: Yeah. Why bother mate? Why? Might as well. Ya know. Drink ya own—

A: And—

AE: Ya own piss.

A: Too right.

AE: Ya know?

A: And in. In bloody. In, ah. Yeah. In bloody London, pubs—

AE: Yeah?

A: Pubs close at eleven! At bloody—

AE: Bullshit!

A: No! No bullshit!

AE: Eleven?

A: Yeah!

AE: That's bullshit.

A: It's true mate. True as—

AE: No, ah, wonder they're all such. Ya know.

A: Yeah.

AE: Miserable fuckin' cunts.

A: Cheers to that mate. Cheers to that.

AE: Yeah.

A / AE:

AE: Ya fight along side some of 'em or somethin'?

A: What?

AE: Over there? You been sittin' on y'arse hearin' stories of the mother country while we've all been thinkin' y've had ya sleeves rolled up and ya arms deep in the enemy's shit?

A: Yeah, something like that.

AE: Miserable fuckin'… ya know?

A: Bloody English beers and bloody English pubs.

A / AE:

AE: Another?

A: Yeah. Got a. Got a ticklish one tonight mate. A real ticklish—

AE: Oh yeah? What's up?

A: Hey?

AE: What's up?

A: Up? Nothing. Just got a. You know. A ticklish bloody throat. Yeah? It's been a while.

AE: Ya bloody chirpy but.

A: Am I?

AE: Yeah. Sure are. Bloody English beers and bloody English pubs and all that. Bloody chirpy is what you are.

A: English beers and English pubs mate.

AE: You. Normally first beer back with ya it's like gettin' bloody blood from a fuckin' rock. But not tonight. Ya get lucky or somethin' ya—

A: Well—

AE: Majesty?

A: You know me, mate. Not one to kiss and tell.

AE: Cheeky bugger. Jeez. Ya get home. Bloody. From fuck knows how long in deserty bloody hell. Ya know. Go home. Have a barbeque with the family. Get lucky. With ya missus. Ya lady. While I sit here all on me lonesome like a loner, waitin' for ya. Then. Ah. Ya come to the fuckin' pub for some Ashes and some bloody beers like nothin's changed? Not a bad bloody day mate. Not a bad bloody day for ya.

A: Yeah but.

AE: But what? Sounds good to me. Sounds bloody good to me.

A: But it's raining at least. You know. It's bloody raining.

AE: Huh? Yeah. Good point. Bloody England and the bloody rain.

A: Yeah.

AE:

A:

AE: So. What's it like, hey? Over there? In the middle of it? It's gotta fuck with ya, doesn't it? Gotta fuck ya in the head a bit bein' over there.

A: Yeah I guess. You know me, mate.

AE: Yeah. I mean ya seem yaself but it's gotta be bloody hard, hey?

A: Sure.

AE: The things ya woulda seen.

A: You're not wrong.

AE: And then to have to come back and be all happy families, that must be pretty hard.

A: Yeah. Too hard for some, you know.

AE: Hard for ya missus too, hey?

A: Yeah. Guess so.

AE: Yeah?

A: Yeah.

AE: Yeah.

A:

AE: Any women, ya know, over there?

A: What?

AE: Did ya see any women? Ya know what I mean? Any foreign beauties that you've brought back to, ya know, be ya trophy? Ya bit on the fuckin' side?

A: What?

AE: Isn't that what you warriors do? Disappear off into the sunset and come back covered in blood with the gorgeous daughter of the beaten enemy king or some bloody thing?

A: Yeah, right.

AE: That's me, cuz.

A: You've seen too many bloody movies mate.

AE: Yeah. Or heard too many stories maybe?

A: Yeah.

A / AE:

AE: So she. She good, is she?

A: Good?

AE: Ya know. Ya missus?

A: Yeah. She's good.

AE: Good to be back with her?

A: Yeah.

AE: She still dunks a good dagwood, does she?

A: Mate.

AE: Just jokin' mate. Just havin' a—

A: Yeah but.

AE: A lend mate.

A: Yeah.

AE: Ya know that.

A: Yeah but. Well. She does me fine. Does me just fine.

AE: Yeah right. Ya missus, hey? Must be hard for her.

A:

AE: She. Ah. Like the tattoo?

A: The—

AE: Ya tattoo? Ya new one?

A: Oh yeah. Yeah. Of course she does. Of course.

AE: That's romantic mate.

A: Yeah nah.

AE: Nah. That's real romantic. Cheers to that.

A: Cheers.

AE: She's a good one that woman of yours.

A: Yeah. You reckon?

AE: Huh?

A: Do you reckon?

AE: For sure. Bloody.

A: Yeah. You know. I guess.

AE: Guess? Ya bloody. Ya better bloody. Hot too. A real hot looker too I reckon.

A: Sure. No doubt there. No doubt at all there.

AE: A real. I remember when. When we all went up to the lakes. Do ya? To the shack. Do ya remember that?

A: Yeah. Way back. Yeah.

AE: Yeah well. I remember when we went up there to the lakes. All those years ago. And she came out in that bikini for a swim. Came out of the shack in that bikini for a swim in the lakes in that. And I remember thinkin'. I gotta say I remember thinkin'. Jesus. Wow. That's a real fuckin'. I mean. Looker I reckon. Is what I thought. I'd like to. I'd really like to sharpen me axe on that piece of—

A: Mate.

AE: Sorry mate. Nah. All respect. I'm just sayin' that up there at the lakes. I know that was a long time ago, but now. Now she's still. Ya know? Still real bloody—

A: Yeah well. Thanks mate. I mean I know. I know she's. But just take a. I mean I tattooed her fucking name on my. So don't think I don't know that she's still gorgeous. Bloody gorgeous. But. But she's the fucking mother of my children, mate, so just watch what you—

AE: Nah. Yeah. Sure mate. Apologies. Just tryin' to. I mean she is. I really reckon she is. Ya know. Ya woman. Well, y've been a lucky man.

A: You reckon?

AE: Oh yeah.

A: Yeah thanks.

AE: Yeah a real lucky man.

A: Yeah.

AE: Cheers to. Cheers to that, hey?

A: Up your arse.

A / AE:

AE: Yeah, I mean. But I hope ya treat her right.

A: Sorry?

AE: Just sayin'.

A: What?

AE: Just sayin' ya gotta do good by those ones. Ya don't wanna treat 'em bad. No way. Like a. I mean I saw that even right back then up at the lakes. Saw that she was one that ya. Ya should treat like a bloody princess. Like a fuckin' goddess is how ya should treat that one. Like they have come straight down from, from fuckin' heaven. Is how ya should respect 'em, ya know? Ya know what I mean?

A: Yeah. Sure. Yeah.

AE: Yeah?

A: Yeah.

AE: Good one. Drink up.

A: Yeah. Cheers.

AE: Cheers.

A: Same again?

AE: Sure.

A: You got a woman, mate?

AE: Me?

A: Yeah.

AE: Nah. Not right now. Nah.

A: Right. Another one then.

A / AE:

AE: They reckon the whole thing. The whole Test might be rained out. How fucked would that be? How fuckin' fucked would that be? The whole Test.

A: Yeah. A bit of a disappointment I reckon. A bit of a bloody disappointment. I mean having the big screen and all and if the whole thing gets rained out that would be a real disappointment. I've been hanging for this. Ever since I knew I was coming home I've been hanging to sit here with you and have a little chat and watch the Ashes on the big screen, but if it's rained out...

AE: Yeah.

A:

AE: But ya do though, don't ya?

A: What?

AE: Sorry. Treat her right.

A: Mate. What are you talking about? What's all this about?

AE: It's not about nothin' it's just. Well this. Well, I know this bird, right. This beautiful fuckin'. I mean. And I reckon. Well, I said I didn't have a woman before but I do. Kind of. And I reckon there's a good chance that I. Ya know. Love her, mate.

A: Oh yeah?

AE: Yeah. She's like a. A bloody. Some kind of. I don't know. I can't even say. Ya know?

A: Yeah. You told me. Said you didn't have one.

AE: Yeah well. The thing is. The only thing is.

A: Yeah?

AE: Well, she's with this other bloke.

A: Oh yeah?

AE: Yeah. And I know about the other bloke, ya know, but. Y'ain't tellin' no one this, are ya? Y'ain't gonna. Nah. But the other bloke mate. He don't know about me.

A: Right.

AE: Right. Well this. This other bloke. Well, I don't know but I don't reckon he treats her too good. Nothin' physical. It's not like I ever see any bruises or nothin' on her. Well, no more than usual. You know how women always have some kinda bruises on 'em? Why is that, hey? On their legs and stuff. Why is it they always seem to have—

A: Mate...

AE: Yeah. Sorry. It's the piss. Well, it's just sometimes. Sometimes when we're lyin' together. Naked. In bed. In their bed. Lyin' in their bed after makin' beautiful fuckin' love. I mean love like I never. Sometimes she talks. Says stuff. Ya know? Like he's been tellin' her stories or somethin'.

A:

AE: And it's probably just dreams. Weird bloody dreams but the stuff she says. That she's told me. Shared with me. That he's made her do. Made her give up and stuff. Well. It's dark, mate. It's bloody dark. And the only thing I can think is that she's gettin' it. Somehow gettin' it from him. Ya know what I mean?

A: Right.

AE: I mean she's not gettin' it from me. I only ever tell her good things. Sweet whispery things because. Ya know. I love her. I've come to love her a lot. And this dark, dark shit is comin' from somewhere and it messes her up mate. Messes her up real bad. Ya know. And I guess what I'm tryin' to say. I mean it must sound weird me harkin' on about it. But what I reckon I'm tryin' to say is if ya love her, ya know? Really love her. Then mate. Ya treat her like a fuckin' princess and don't give her nothin' to be dark about. Whatever it takes. Okay? Ya hear me? Do ya hear me, mate?

A: Yeah.

AE: Because I've got a right mind. If this bloke has done somethin' to me princess. Me queen goddess. I don't care if she was his first. I reckon I might be inclined to climb in through his window in the middle of the night while he's lyin' next to her and slice his fuckin' dick off with me leatherman. Ya know? Him and whoever he is no doubt fuckin' behind her back.

A: Look. Are you? Are you trying to tell me something here? Are you talking about me here? Because if you're not. If you're not mate. Why are you laying all this out to me? I mean if you're talking about someone else then why the hell are you bloody laying all this out like this to me, hey? Hey mate?

AE: Mate?

A: Hey cousin?

AE: Because ya me blood and me mate.

A: Yeah?

AE: Yeah. Of course. Yeah.

A: You're not bullshitting me because I remember. I remember the way you looked at her up at the shack that time. At the lakes. Way back then. I remember you two going off in the boat. Going off in the bloody tinny together and when you came back she was. She was all. And it's not like you ain't jealous about everything I've got to have and you've missed out on. I mean it's not like you ain't completely fucking jealous. Even though we are mates. That we've worked hard to get it behind us and be mates. It's not like it's out of the realms of fucking possibility that you would get it in your head to fall for my woman just to get back at me. At me. So you should tell me if you're bullshitting me here.

AE: I've been fuckin' ya woman.

A: What?

AE: Ever since you went off to war after sendin' her off to the city for a bit I've been livin' in ya home and sleeping in ya bed and fuckin' ya wife and I love 'er.

A: You what? You fucking—

AE: And don't tell me this is jealousy. That what I'm doin' is jealousy just because I know how to love her better than you do, because she's told me. She's told me all about ya.

A: What the fuck? You better watch what you—

AE: And I'm in love with 'er and she has told me what ya do to 'er.

A: Fuck you. Fuck you, you're fucking my woman! What I do to her? What I have done? You sit there. You fucking sit there and you tell me you're fucking my woman and then make it sound like it's my? I mean, jesus! Fucking—

AE: Yeah that's right. She's told me everythin' and I have a right mind to take out me leatherman right here. Right here mate and slice ya dirty balls right off ya. I don't care what kinda hero ya reckon y'are. Ya know that?

A: Fuck you mate. You try. You fucking. I can't believe this. You? But you're my. You say that you're in love. In fucking love?

AE: Yeah. And she told me what you did to her, ya sick. Ya fuckin' sick little—

A: What I? What did I do to her, then? What did I? What I do mate. What I do with my woman in my house is none of your. None of your fucking—

AE: She told me how ya—

A: None of your fucking business! What I fucking do is none of your fucking business you piece of—

AE: How ya do 'er up the arse and—

A: You better. You better shut the fuck—

AE: Do her up the arse and call 'er by my name.

A: You better just fucking—

AE: Do 'er up the arse and call 'er by my fuckin' name!

A: What?

AE: I mean we're mates and all. But that, mate? That's a bit. I mean we're bloody related.

A: You said what? She said. You're fucking with me. You're winding me up.

AE: I mean if ya wanna fuck me, mate. Fuck me up the arse. All ya had to do was bloody—

A: You're winding me up.

AE: Ya just have to bloody ask mate.

A: You...

AE: When it's rainin' in the Ashes ya gotta entertain yaself somehow.

A: You reckon that's funny?

AE: I sure do! Ya face, cuz! Ya face is priceless!

A: You reckon it's funny for you to joke about me like that?

AE: I've been savin' that one up for months! As if I'd wanna stir your fucking custard!

A: You reckon it's funny for you to joke about my woman like that?

AE: Mate?

A:

AE: Yeah, but. I mean. Mate.

A: You reckon that's funny?

AE: I was. I was just…

A:

AE: I was…

A:

AE: I didn't mean—

A: Didn't mean what?

AE:

A: Didn't mean what, mate?

AE:

A: Cousin?

AE: Nothin'.

A: Didn't mean nothing?

AE: Nah.

A: Right.

AE:

A: That's a double negative you dumb cunt.

AE:

A: What was that all about?

AE: Just. Just havin' a lend mate. Leadin' you on. Ya know? I was just…

A:

AE:

A: My dad did the right fucking thing taking the farm. You're just like your father was. A pair of dumb fucking cunts.

AE: Ma—

A: Fuck this. They still got that karaoke machine round here somewhere?

AE: Sorry?

A: I feel like a fucking sing.

AE: Mate?

A: What?

AE:

A: Nothing to say?

AE:

A: Up your arse, little brother cousin.

AE / A:

A: Right. Time for a fucking sing then.

SCENE FIVE

We see C.

C: The lights of the ute. The brakes. The wheels in the gravel driveway. The door. Him coming home. I was waiting because I hadn't seen him in a long time. I hadn't been alone with him in so long. I wanted to wait up to be there for him for his first night in our bed. In our. But he was yelling. Then. I don't know. He must have. I think he must have kicked the door in because it just. It just flew open and he was yelling. Loud. At me. He pulled my. I was sitting in the kitchen and he came in and he grabbed me and he pulled my hair back with his fist. He shoved his other fist. His tattooed fist in my face and spat in my face as he yelled at me to read what was on his fist. The tattoo. He swore. He said. Sorry. But he screamed read what's on my fucking fist. I'm sorry to swear but. He screamed at me, you know? Spat in my face and I was. He screamed to read what was on his fucking. His fist and I knew, you see? It was. I could read it. Sorry. His fist because it was my name. A different letter on each finger. He came back from the war and there it was. My name. He punched me in the face. I think. The ambulance man said he thinks he broke my nose and then he picked me up and yelled at me. Called me a bitch. A cheating. Pushes me into the fridge. Then onto the table that I think must have broken because then I was on the floor. He sat on my chest. On my breasts. Then he picked my head up and slammed it into the floor. Over and over. He was also hitting me. Again and again. And I didn't know what. It was so. One minute the ute's pulling up and the next I am on the floor and he is slamming my head into the tiles and hitting. Hitting me in the. Over and over. And the tattoo. That tattoo. I could see it. See it come down each. And he yelled and yelled and I couldn't say anything and then I... then I...

She pauses for a moment. Silent. She then hums a little of the tune of 'I Am Woman' by Helen Reddy to herself. After a little humming, she mumbles her way through the chorus, trailing off before the end of the final chorus line.

She pauses for another short moment, before...

I went black. My vision all went black and I could feel the thuds but couldn't. Then it stopped. He stopped. He got off. I felt him. He got off and walked to the bathroom and ran himself a bath and got in and lit a cigarette and I knew because I could hear it. I could hear those sounds. I knew them. Knew what they were if you know what I. I mean I had heard them so many times before and. And everything was still black and I was so. I don't know. I got up. I got up and went to the bedroom and got his gun. His 303 he uses for roo shooting. I got it and walked to the bathroom and I barely knew what I was doing. Like a zombie or something, you know? And he was sitting there smoking. His hands all. There was blood everywhere. In the kitchen. On the floor. On his clothes in a pile. On his hands. And he turned to me and I had his gun and I don't know. He said sorry before he started hitting me he said sorry like he. Like he knew I was going to do this. That I was going to. And he looked at me and I. Before I know what I shoot him. I shot him. I shot him in the head. I don't know. I feel. I mean I didn't mean. I don't know why I. I shot him right there in the bath three times and then. Then I called you straight away. I called you, officer, straight away. I shot him. I really. I mean I never ever thought I could do something like that but he hit me so bad. He. I didn't know what was. I was in a daze and there was so much blood and then I shot him. I shot him officer. Is he? Is he okay? Is he?

SCENE SIX

We see C and AE.

C: He, ah—

AE: Yes?

C: He held my hair back.

AE: Yes…

C: Caressed. He caressed it back with his hand.

AE: No.

C: What?

AE: How?

C: How? With his—

AE: Yes his hand or his—

C: Sorry, I don't—

AE: Or his—

C: I don't—

AE: With his hand, yes, or his fist?

AE *demonstrates.*

C: No. Why would he—

AE: Because. Well. Was he in a caressin' mood?

C: Yes. Yes he was in a caressing mood.

AE: Okay.

C: He caressed my hair back with his hand.

AE: Okay.

C: He softly caressed my hair back with his hand.

AE: Softly? Right. He softly caressed ya hair back with his hand. And?

C: He said—

AE: Said?

C: Yes.

AE: Not whisper?

C: No.

AE: He wasn't. Ya know. I mean caressin' and everythin'. So he wasn't suddenly all lovin'. All whisperin' and lovin' as well?

C: No. Not yet. He softly caressed my hair back. Yes. Softly. But like it could be a friend or a father or something. He was not yet all loving like that. Not yet.

AE: And?

C: He asked 'can we do this?'

AE: Meanin'…

C: The story I had just told him.

AE: The story y'd just told him…

C: Yes.

AE: That y'd read in one of ya husband's old school textbooks…

C: Yes.

AE: About?

C: About a warrior king arriving home…

AE: Yes?

C: From war…

AE: Yes?

C: To have his wife…

AE: Yes?

C: To have his wife…

AE:

C: You know….

AE: Kill him?

C: Yes.

AE: Right. Good. That's good. And ya said?

C: I said yes. Yes we could.

AE: Ya could?

C: Yes.

AE: Ya could. That's what ya said. Right. Then what did he say?

C: How.

AE: No, what did he say—

C: No. He said how. He asked. He softly caressed my hair back with his hand. Not yet completely loving, but getting close. Intimate. Definitely intimate. And he asked 'can we do this?' and then 'how are we going to do this?'

AE: And did ya answer him? Do ya know how ya gonna do it?

C: Yes I do. It is my idea. My plan. My husband. Yes I certainly do know how we're going to do it.

AE: Ya do know.

C: And now I've told him so now we must do it.

AE: But…

C: We must!

AE: But…

C: He said no. He wouldn't. He refused.

AE: Why?

C: He said it isn't right.

AE: Why isn't it right?

C: I don't know.

AE: Not 'I don't know'.

C: But—

AE: Is it right for her. For the wife. The beautiful wife. To have to do that? Do all that? And he. The man. The… And he just has to stand back and not act?

C: Yes.

AE: Is that right?

C: Yes!

AE: Come on.

C: Aren't we past that, though? Me and him?

AE: Past it? You go to him. You tell him all this and then you're both supposed to just be—

C: Aren't we? I mean. Sure. He can ask it. Ask it again. Ask it as many times as he needs to, but really. Really. Aren't we past that? Can't he see a way around that?

AE: Around it?

C: Yes.

AE: His cousin…

C: Yes, his—

AE: And you…

C: Yes. Me.

AE: And you expect him just to sit back? To bloody sit back and do what you—

C: Yes. Yes I expect that. Okay? Okay? I expect him to hear me out. To listen. To really listen to what I. Then accept it. Then softly caress my hair back and… because… because this is. This is about both of us, yes? I mean this is about—

AE: Okay.

C: Yes?

AE: Okay. So he didn't refuse. Okay. Right. You're right. He was past that. He was completely one hundred percent true-blue past that. He didn't kick up a fuss, he didn't sit there listenin' to all of this and then suddenly. Like real suddenly rush over to ya and pull ya hair back. Just to. Just to get ya bloody attention and shout at ya. Scream at ya to stop all this fuckin' craziness that is messin' with his head. To just stop fuckin' talkin' for a moment. For a fuckin' second. He didn't do that. Instead he just softly caressed ya hair back with his hand and he asked ya if ya can do this and ya said yes and he asked ya how were ya gonna do this and ya told him. Ya told him and he accepted it. Right. Okay. Is that about right?

C:

AE: Or maybe he should've. To be sure. Just to get it out of his bloody system. Maybe he should've rushed over to ya and. And told ya to shut the. To shut up with all that fuckin' craziness because it was. It was, ya see. It was doin' his fuckin' head in! Perhaps he should've done that!

C: No.

AE: He's his cousin. He's his bloody—

C: Don't play that. Don't even start to. Because that. That is. That is bullshit. That is absolutely. And he—

AE: Bullshit?

C: Yes. Bullshit. And he knew it because—

AE: He knew it?

C: Yes!

AE: How did he know it? How did he know that it's bullshit?

C: You need me to tell you?

AE: Yes!

C: You need me to tell you why he couldn't pull that 'he's my cousin' shit and get away with it?

AE: Yes! Yes I need ya to… Ya better believe I need ya to tell me why he couldn't pull—

C: Because if he didn't, yes?

AE: Yeah?

C: If he didn't know that that was complete bullshit.

AE: Yeah? If he didn't fuckin'—

C: Then he fucking wouldn't fucking have been here, would he?

AE:

C: He would never have fucking come here, would he? Fucking come into this home. Like that. Would he? He would never fucking have become my fucking lover, would he?

AE: Jesus.

C: 'His cousin'…

AE: Jesus fuckin'… Fuck. Sorry to… for sayin'…Okay. I'm sorry. I'm so sorry ba—

C: Don't call me that.

AE: Baby?

C: Don't.

AE / C:

AE: Then… sorry but… then what did you do? You and him?

C: Sorry?

AE: Then what?

C: Then? We kissed.

AE: Ya kissed?

C: Yes.

AE: So now he was all lovin'? Suddenly he was—

C: He was building. He had begun to build to being all loving. Yes.

AE: Right.

C: He put his other hand. Yes? Open hand. On my neck and cheek and. And told me… sorry…

AE: It's okay.

C: He softly caressed my hair back with his hand and kissed me and then put his other hand. His other open hand on my neck and cheek and said—

AE: Did he? Maybe? Did he whisper then?

C: Sorry?

AE: It's just. I'm tryin' here, okay? I'm really tryin' and I can see what ya about to say and. And I'm really tryin' to hold a lot of shit back here and get to the middle of this to be there. To be there with ya. So. Did he say or did he maybe whisper?

C: Whisper?

AE: Yes.

C: No.

AE: You know how. Whisper. Up close.

C: No I don't—

AE: Because ya know how people can. In moments like that. In. I'm tryin', yeah? In intimate moments like that. And we ain't. I'm pretty sure we ain't disputin' that it was an intimate moment, are we?

C: No.

AE: I mean caresses and plans of doin' those things and everythin' so…

C: Yes.

AE: Well, ya know how people. In moments like that. In intimate moments like that people can whisper? Even when they don't need to. They still for some reason whisper. Ya know?

C: No. But. I know. I know how in moments like that. Intimate moments people can whisper. But he. He said. He said it clearly and strongly because he had a lot. A rage of things going through his head and that was okay, yes? That rage of things was completely okay, yes? But he. He wanted to be clear. Okay?

AE: Okay.

C: So he caressed my hair and kissed me and held my neck and cheek and looked into my eyes and said that he—

AE: Wait. Sorry. But. I know that we are. That I said I knew what you were gonna say. But. Are you sure? Is that the? Because. You know. Isn't that a little obvious? To say that then? For the first. After all—

C: What?

AE: Sayin' that. After all that. Isn't that a little bit too obvious?

C: Fuck you.

AE: Okay.

C: Obvious? I mean fucking—

AE: Okay.

C: He held me. Caressed my hair back and held me and we talked about. About doing this together. Because those letters... you know this... those letters that I had got from my—

AE: Yes, I know, but—

C: From my husband were... were desperate. Were horrible and desperate and it was clear, it was pretty damn clear what he wanted, yes?

AE: I know what ya sayin', but—

C: So I had found that story and read it to my... my lover and we had talked about all this and it was hard and we talked through the night and we finally got to a point of understanding. Where I could write out the story and send it. Post it to my husband as a... like as a reply to what he had... the things he had been telling me, and that is a hard thing. A very hard thing to do so my lover put all the shit aside and saw the sacrifice I was making and what it would mean for the two of us and he fucking well caressed my hair and kissed me and held me and told me that he loved—

AE: Good. Okay. Sure. Okay. And are ya gonna?

C: Write the—

AE: Write the letter?

C: Of course I am going to write the fucking—

AE: Because. Ya know. That's it. It sounds like once that is written and sent then that is it.

C: Of course I—

AE: Because if you do this. You and ya lover. If ya do write this down and send this to ya husband then there is only one way this can go. He's gonna know, yeah? Ya husband? He will read it and in readin' it he's gonna know, so whatever. Whatever he thinks about it from that moment there is only one way this can go. You and ya lover need to think about that I reckon. It sounds to me like ya need to really think about that because there is no. Because, ya know, there is no turnin' back from that point if ya—

C: Know? Do I? Yes. Fucking yes. Yes I know. Okay? Because if we do this. If we send this and he reads it and he does what I think he will do which is say 'nice letter', yes? Nice story, yes? Even then if we are to have this. If we are to get what we. Me and my... What we deserve from him then we are going to have to go through him first because he can't be seen to. Can't be seen to just lie down and... because he is not a weak man and he can't be seen to end it with such a, he has said this in his letters to me, such a weak act. Because of all that, I am going to have to do this. What we talked about. All those things we talked about as being the only way we can do this. I'm going to have to go through that while he... my lover... while he is off. Off twiddling his thumbs or something so don't. Don't you...

AE:

C: Do I know!

AE: Jesus.

C: Yes, jesus. Fucking hell.

AE: So. Ya talked about all that. Ya spent all night talkin'. Until the sun. Until the sun was back up in the sky. Like ya had talked since it went down all the way until when it came up again and ya battled and raged and held and hoped and did all those bloody things because of what ya were talkin' about and then. Then as the sun was comin' up. He caressed ya hair. Softly. He asked ya can ya do this. Ya said yes. He asked ya how could ya do this. Ya told him. Ya took him through it. Where he had to do nothin'. Had to sit on his bloody hands and do nothin'. And he accepted that. It was bloody hard but somehow he accepted that and he kissed ya and he held ya neck and ya cheek and he said... he told ya that... that he...

C: Yes.

AE: But...

C: What?

AE: Sorry, but…

C: What?

AE: It's just. I'm really hearin' what you just said, okay? But I reckon there's maybe one more thing before he can say that. I reckon there's one other thing he's gotta ask ya—

C: No.

AE: Before he can… It's just. Well. Before he can do that he has to…

C: What? 'Before he can do that he has to' what?

AE: It's just. Ya haven't. Ya haven't talked about. Ya haven't asked each other if it isn't just. Ya know. Two people. Two people in desperate bloody need for some bloody revenge to years and years of dark fuckin' stuff. It's not like y've asked that of each other.

C: Sorry?

AE: And I've. I really have heard eveythin' y've said and I am right. I am right there with ya all the way, I promise. I completely promise that I… But that word is a big word and it means a hell of a lot. Especially considerin'… considerin' all this and so I would think he might wanna ask that first to be sure. To be completely sure. Yeah?

C: Are you… are you kidding me here?

AE: Because. I mean. For him. For him with you it's. It feels so. I mean every bloody thing feels more… that's what he thinks about. Day and night. That you. He thinks that you are like this. This angel that has come from… from… But that doesn't mean there isn't also a ragin' bloody need in him to walk up behind his cousin one day and whisper that he's hated bein' his cousin's bloody 'everythin' is all right' chum mate and call his cousin a dirty fuckin' arse fucker and stab his cousin in the fuckin' back with his leatherman. It's not like that isn't also in him. Now that you tell me I know he can't pull any of that cousin bullshit. And those two things. Two ways of feelin' are really battlin' inside him and it's fuckin'… sorry… fuckin' hard for him to know which one is true. Which one is leadin' him through this. So… so I think it is somethin' worth askin'. Before the two of ya can just kiss and make up. Don't you?

C: This is the time to say that? This is the time he says that? There's no. He doesn't have to be all macho, you know? There's no need, because he feels helpless and maybe a bit. A little bit relieved. Relieved that he doesn't have to... There's no reason why now he has to behave all macho.

AE: I know. But. I mean. I mean he said that. He told ya that he... that he... He said that word before y'd asked each other this question?

C: Yes he did.

AE: Because I don't know—

C: Yes he did!

AE: I don't know if he could. If he could get fuckin' past all that until he had looked ya. Looked ya right in the fuckin' eyes and asked ya that question because. Because isn't that a good bloody question to ask?

C: No. No that is not a good question to—

AE: It's not?

C: No it's—

AE: Well. Sorry. But—

C: No.

AE: But too fuckin' bad.

C: What?

AE: Too fuckin' bad.

C: No. Not too fucking bad! No! Revenge? Revenge? Like that is. Like that is going to help to... to do... Like asking that is going to help to do any fucking thing at all? No! Fucking no! No he does not ask that! He does not need to look me in the eyes and ask... and ask... No. No! Fucking no!

AE:

C: No!

AE: What do ya say?

C:

AE: What's ya answer?

C:

AE: Is it love and not just a means to fuckin' revenge?

C:

AE: Is it?

C:

AE: Well?

C:

AE: Right.

C:

AE: Are ya all right?

C:

AE: Are ya—

C: Yes I'm all right. Just sit for a bit.

AE: Sit here?

C: Yes.

AE: With ya?

C: Yes. With me.

AE: Okay. Hold. Do ya want me to hold ya—

C: Just sit.

AE: Right.

C:

AE: And ya sure? Sorry, but… ya sure of this?

C: Sure?

AE: This will be it, ya know? This will really be it.

C: Yes. This will be it.

AE: Because ya can. Ya can still not do. Ya don't have ta do this, ya know. Ya know? We don't…

C: We don't have to?

AE: No.

C: We don't have to do this?

AE: No. No we don't. We can still—

C: Are you kidding me?

AE: Ya can…

C:

AE: Jesus.

C:

AE: This is it, baby. This is really—

C: Really. Don't call me that.

AE: But—

C: I am not your baby.

AE:

C:

AE: The other day, right, I was on the farm and there was this sheep that was really fightin' hard against me. I mean kickin' and bitin' and all that shit. They always do, ya know? But this one… but there was somethin' about this one that really pissed me off and I thought. Ya know. For a second I thought about beatin' its fuckin' head in with a metal pole. Of grabbin' a metal pole and beatin' its fuckin' head to a pulp. Because it was pissin' me off. I didn't do it, ya know. But in that flash of… of… fucking whatever, I thought about doin' it and in thinkin' about it I felt I kinda knew at least a bit of what it would be like to do it. That shook me up a bit, ya know? Because if I can daydream doin' it, doesn't that mean that it is in me? That violence? That flash of fuckin' violence? The fact that I didn't do it doesn't make much bloody difference really, does it? Because, either way, I know it and that means I am not who I think I am. I am the opposite of who I think I am and everythin' I do is just camouflage to hide that other real bloody me. I am the sort of guy that would beat an innocent fuckin' sheep to death with a metal pole just because it doesn't like me shavin' it nude. Don't ya see?

C:

AE: And ya know what makes it really bloody hard?

C: What?

AE: I mean do ya know what I'm tryin' to say?

C: What?

AE: I bloody love sheep.

C:

AE: Do ya see?

C: Really?

AE: Yes. I think. Really. So if we're gonna do this, yeah? If we're really gonna bloody do it we need to be sure it's not just a bloody thought, yeah?

C: Yeah.

A: So?

C: I don't.

AE: Don't what?

C: I don't love sheep. Not anymore.

AE:

C: And you're not.

AE: Not what?

C: Someone who could beat a sheep to death.

AE: I'm not.

C: There's a difference.

AE / C:

> AE *goes up to* C. *He caresses her hair with his hand.*

AE: Can we do this?

C: Yes we can.

AE: How?

C: Like we said.

>AE *kisses* C.

>*Is it a long passionate kiss? Is it distracted and hesitant?*

>*Once he has kissed her, no matter what kind of kiss it is, he moves his other hand and holds her neck and face.*

AE: I…

C: Yes?

AE:

SCENE SEVEN

We see A. *He has clearly been shot in the head. He struggles from the wound. He sings the last two choruses and verse of 'History Never Repeats', ending on the line about a change of heart.*

THE END

GRIFFIN THEATRE COMPANY AND THE TASMANIAN THEATRE
COMPANY PRESENT THE WORLD PREMIERE OF

Don't Say the Words
by Tom Holloway

Cast

A   **Jack Finsterer**
C   **Anna Lise Phillips**
Ae   **Brett Stiller**

Production

Director	**Matthew Lutton**
Dramaturg	**Peter Matheson**
Designer	**Adam Gardnir**
Lighting Designer	**Paul Jackson**
Composer / Sound Designer	**Kelly Ryall**
Production Manager	**Miles Thomas**
Stage Manager	**Jenn Blake**

Griffin Theatre Company's season of *Don't Say the Words* opened at the SBW Stables Theatre, Sydney on 2 July 2008.

Cover photo by Olivia Martin-McGuire.

Griffin Theatre Company would like to dedicate this production to the memory o: Dr Rodney Seaborn AO OBE

Griffin Theatre Company's long-standing patron, Dr. Rodney Seaborn, passed away on Saturday 17th May, aged ninety-six.

A man whose philanthropic acts provided so much to Sydney's cultural life, Dr. Seaborn is perhaps most well-known for his involvement with Griffin and the SBW Stables Theatre.

Back in 1986, the Stables Theatre, a venue that had played such a critical part in the early life of Nimrod Theatre Company before becoming the home of Griffin Theatre Company, was scheduled for demolition. A public campaign was launched to save the theatre, led by actor Penny Cook.

Dr. Seaborn, a retired Macquarie Street psychiatrist, responded, gathering together a team including Dr. Peter Broughton, Leslie Walford, Anthony Larkins and barrister Lloyd Waddy to form the Seaborn, Broughton and Walford Foundation.

The newly created foundation then bought and restc the Stables Theatre, before allowing Griffin to remain tl rent free (less outgoings) from that moment on.

This visionary act of Australian philanthropy could not H come at a more opportune moment – within 18 months, k Michael Gow's *Away* and Richard Barrett's *The Heartb* *Kid* had premiered at this 120-seat theatre in Kings Cr Griffin Theatre Company was on track once more.

Since 1986, the Seaborn Broughton and Wal Foundation has continued its wide-ranging philanthrc activities – assisting companies including Griffin, but a the Independent Theatre, Company B, Bell Shakespe Company, the Ensemble Theatre and most rece NIDA, and the new SBW / NIDA Archives & Perform Arts Collection.

Griffin would like to pay tribute to Dr. Seaborn – a i whose individual contribution made such a difference so many. He will be missed by us all.

Nick Marchand
Artistic Director

Griffin Theatre Company

The SBW Stables Theatre

ffin Theatre Company is one of the great engine rooms
he Australian theatre and the only theatre company in
dney entirely dedicated to the professional development
production of new plays by Australian writers.

ot-for-profit company that has operated successfully
ce 1978, Griffin offers an annual subscription season
4 to 6 new plays at the SBW Stables Theatre and
ularly tours its productions throughout Australia. In
ition to its education program, Griffin encourages
w writing through an annual playwrights' award, offers a
ywrights' Residency and presents Griffin Stablemates
an annual theatre season of independent theatre
ductions.

ffin Theatre Company has always been a place of good
ginnings. Many artists who began professional careers
h the Company now contribute significantly to the
stralian theatre, film and television industries, including
te Blanchett and Jacqueline McKenzie. The hit films
ntana and *The Boys* began life as plays first produced
Griffin, as did the TV series *Heartbreak High*. Many
er plays premiered by Griffin are produced regularly
oughout Australia and internationally, including *Holding
Man*, *Clark in Sarajevo*, *Wolf Lullaby* and Australia's
st produced play, *Away*.

Griffin is the resident theatre company at the historic
SBW Stables Theatre and is proud to curate the venue on
behalf of its owner, the Seaborn, Broughton and Walford
Foundation. In 2008, the theatre will host five Griffin
season productions as well as five Griffin Stablemates
collaborations and other events.

GRIFFIN THEATRE COMPANY
13 Craigend Street, Kings Cross NSW 2011
Phone: 9332 1052
Fax: 9331 1524
Email: info@griffintheatre.com.au
Web: www.griffintheatre.com.au

SBW STABLES THEATRE
10 Nimrod Street, Kings Cross NSW 2011
Bookings: 1300 306 776
or online at
www.griffintheatre.com.au

Tom Holloway
Playwright

For **Griffin Theatre Company**: Debut. **Other theatre**: For Royal Court Theatre, London and Tasmania Performs/A Bit Of Argy Bargy, Tasmania: *Beyond the Neck*. For Red Stitch Actors Theatre: *Red Sky Morning*. For ABC Radio National, *The Bus*. For La Mama: *Pathetique and the Papers/Snarl*. For Naked Theatre Company: *Stones In My Passway*. **Positions:** Playwright-in-Residence at Red Stitch Actors Theatre in Melbourne, Playwright-in-Residence RAG Theatre Troupe in Melbourne. Arts Hub columnist. **Training:** NIDA and the Royal Court Theatre, London.

Matthew Lutton
Director

For **Griffin Theatre Company**: Debut. **Other theatre**: **As Director:** For Malthouse Theatre: *Tartuffe*. For Black Swan Theatre Company/Perth International Arts Festival 2007: *The Lady Aoi*. For Be Active BSX-Theatre: *Woyzeck, The Visit, Mountain Language, Striptease*. For ThinIce: *The Goose Chase, The Gathering, Bed, The Bald Prima Donna*. **As Assistant Director:** For Company B: *Toy Symphony*. For Sydney Theatre Company: *The Bourgeois Gentleman*. For West Australian Opera: *The Magic Flute*. **Positions:** Current Board Member for Theatre Board of the Australia Council for the Arts, the Artistic Director of ThinIce. Former Black Swan Theatre Company's Associate Director and Artistic Director of their Be Active BSX-Theatre program. **Awards:** Best Production at the Perth International Fringe Festival 2003 for *The Bald Prima Donna*, Best Production at the 2005 Equity Guild Awards for *The Visit*, a Young People and the Arts Fellowship from ArtsWA (2007) and Young West Australian of the Year for Arts in 2005.

Jack Finsterer
A

For **Griffin Theatre Company**: *The Emperor of Sydney, The Woman with Dog's Eyes*. **Other theatre**: For Elston Hocking & Woods: *Romeo & Juliet*. For Keene/Taylor Project: *Beneath Heaven, The Share, The Choir Book*. For Playbox Theatre: *Jungfrau, Disturbing the Dust*. For Sydney Theatre Company: *Cyrano de Bergerac, Third World Blues, Titus Andronicus*. **Film:** *In Her Skin, Kokoda, Preservation, Strange Fits of Passion, Five Guys in a Car*. **TV:** *Dangerous, All Saints, Big Reef, Jessica, The Lost World, McLeod's Daughters, Love is a Four Letter Word, Stingers, Good Guys Bad Guys, Janus, The Man from Snowy River*. **Training:** Victorian College of the Arts. Jack is a Proud Member of Equity.

Anna Lise Phillips
C

For Griffin Theatre Company: Debut. **Other theatre:** For Brink Productions: *When The Rain Stops Falling*. For Company B: *The Spook, Gates of Egypt, Rhinoceros*. For Melbourne Theatre Company: *Sweet Bird of Youth*. For Sydney Theatre Company: *Festen*. For Two Hour Traffic: *52 Pick Up*. For Black Swan Theatre: *Popcorn*. **Film:** *Walking on Water, Envy, The Boys, Willful, A-Wreck-A-Tangle, Wanted*. **TV**: *Bastard Boys, Young Lions, The Secret Life of Us* (Series 2), *McLeod's Daughters, Backberner, The Three Stooges, Marriage Acts, FARSCAPE, Stingers, Heartbreak High, A Difficult Woman, Murder Call, Good Guys Bad Guys, Water Rats, Wildside, Big Sky*. **Awards:** 2002 AFI Nomination for Best Film Actress in a Supporting Role – *Envy*. Training: NIDA.

Brett Stiller
AE

For Griffin Theatre Company: *Holding the Man* (SBW Stables Theatre, Company B, Brisbane Powerhouse, Melbourne Theatre Company and Sydney Opera House seasons), *Strangers in Between* (2005), *Borderlines*. **Other theatre**: For Sydney Theatre Company: *The Miser, Falsettos*. For Wharf2Loud/STC: *Stag*. For Glen Street Theatre Company: *Bash – Latterday Plays*. For Theatre Nepean: *Richard II, Traitors, The Man from Mukinupin, Playboy of the Western World, Alice's Adventures Underground*. **Film:** *Travelling Light, Garage Days*. **Short Film:** *Checkpoint, The Manual, Still Life, The Visitor*. **TV:** *City Homicide, The Alice* (Series 1), *The Alice* (Telemovie), *All Saints, The Postcard Bandit, Farscape, Water Rats*. **Training:** Theatre Nepean, The Lee Strasberg Theatre & Film Institute New York.

Adam Gardnir
Designer

For Griffin Theatre Company: Debut. **Other theatre:** For Griffin Stablemates: *Mercury Fur.* Company B: *Paul* (Set). For Malthouse Theatre: *A View of Concrete, The Autobiography of Red, The Yellow Wallpaper, Drink Pepsi, Bitch!* For Stuck Pigs Squealing: *The Eisteddfod* (Melbourne, Sydney & New York), *Volcano*. **Opera:** For OzOpera: *The Beggar's Opera, The Little Sweep.* For Melbourne Opera: *Die Fledermaus.* For Victorian Opera: *Rembrandt's Wife.* **Musical:** For Echeleon Productions: *Virgins* (Melbourne & New York). **Dance:** For The Australian Ballet: *Interplay.* For Ox Dance: *Open Space Hotel.* **Film:** *The Tragedy of Hamlet, Prince of Denmark* (MIFF '07) and several short films. **Awards:** Nominations for Best Design Green Room Awards in 2005, 2006 and 2007. **Training:** Victorian College of the Arts.

Peter Matheson
Dramaturg

For Griffin Theatre Company: Debut. **Other theatre**: As Dramaturg for: ANPC (Residency Programs 2003, 2004, 2005, 2006), Australian Script Centre, Brink Productions, Darwin Theatre Company, Kite Theatre Company, Kooemba Jdarra Indigenous Theatre Company, JUTE (2006/07/08 Enter Stage Write Programs), La Boite, Legs on the Wall (for the 2004 Sydney Festival), Northern Rivers Writers Centre, Playlab, QPAC (for the 2004 Out of the Box Festival), QTC (for their Emerging Writers Program and the Queensland Premier's Drama Awards), Red Dust Theatre, Alice Springs and Street Theatre, Canberra. **Positions:** Dramaturg-in-residence at Playlab, Teacher of Playwriting at ANPC and 2007 Ubud Writers Festival.

Paul Jackson
Lighting Designer

For Griffin Theatre Company: Debut. **Other theatre**: As Lighting Designer: includes The Australian Ballet, Royal New Zealand Ballet, Melbourne Theatre Company, West Australian Ballet, Playbox, Malthouse Theatre, Ballet Lab, not yet it's difficult performance group, Oz Opera, Chamber Made Opera and many others. **As Lecturer in design:** University of Melbourne, RMIT University, NMIT and Victorian College of the Arts. **Positions:** Theatre, Architectural and Events Lighting Designer for The Flaming Beacon. Current Artist-in-Residence at Malthouse Theatre. A co-founder and technical manager of the not yet it's difficult performance group, **Awards:** Gilbert Spottiswood Churchill Fellow for 2007. Victorian Green Room Awards – Best Lighting (Opera) Award for 2004, Best Design (Cabaret) 2005 and Best Lighting (Drama) 2006.

Kelly Ryall
Composer/Sound Designer
For **Griffin Theatre Company**: Debut. **Other theatre**: For The Amazing Business: *Chocolate Monkey* and *Spacemunki, Love Monkey*. For Angus Cerini's Doubletap: *Chapters from the Pandemic* and *Detest*. For the Black Hole Theatre Company: *Coop*. For the Hothouse Theatre Company: *The Glory*. For little death and Griffin Stablemates: *Mercury Fur*. For Platform Youth Theatre: *Tenderness*. For The Town Bikes: *The Meat Show*. For UHT: *Attempts on Her Life*. **Positions:** Co-founder of the Amazing Business, an Artistic Associate of the Storeroom Theatre Workshop and a musician with band High Pass Filter. **Awards:** 2007 Melbourne International Festival Award (*Spacemunki* & *Small Revolutions*), 2005 Green Room Award, Fringe Award, 2008 Nomination for Green Room Award (*Chapters from the Pandemic*).

Miles Thomas
Production Manager
For **Griffin Theatre Company**: *The Nightwatchman, October, The Story of the Miracles at Cookie's Table, King Tide, China, Impractical Jokes* and *The Kid*. **Other theatre**: For Old Fitzroy Hotel Theatre: *Woomera, Woyeck*. For SUDS: *Into the Woods*. For Red Phone Theatre: *Strangelove: The Musical*. **Positions:** Production Co-ordinator for Paris Opera Ballet: Sydney tour 2007. Production Manager for Griffin Theatre Company. Lighting Technician and Head Electrician for Sydney Theatre Company, the Seymour Centre and the Capitol Theatre.

Jenn Blake
Stage Manager
For **Griffin Theatre Company**: Debut. **Other theatre**: Include for Bell Shakespeare: *Romeo & Juliet*. For Big hART Productions: *Stickybricks*. For Company B: *Exit the King*. For Marguerite Pepper Productions: *This Show Is About People*. For Performance Space: *Back From Front*. For Priscilla On Stage: *Priscilla The Musical*. **Positions:** Production & Exhibition Assistant *Sculpture by the Sea* Bondi 2006 & 2007 and Bosco Theatre Venue Manager Melbourne Comedy Festival 2007 & Adelaide Fringe Festival 2007 & 2008. **Training:** NIDA

Tasmanian TheatreCo.

The Tasmanian Theatre Company is proud to co-produce Tom Holloway's *Don't Say the Words* with Griffin Theatre Company.

The Tasmanian Theatre Company is Tasmania's flagship theatre company. The TTC produces contemporary Australian theatre and focuses on telling Tasmanian stories and promoting the work of Tasmanian artists.

The Tasmanian Theatre Company commissions and produces new plays, tours throughout Tasmania and undertakes training with Tasmanian Theatre artists.

In addition the TTC operates a Community Enrichment Program which works with indigenous performers, emerging artists, young people and disabled performers.

Visit tastheatre.com for the latest Tasmanian Theatre Company news, production information, online bookings and email updates.

Griffin Theatre Company

rd Hilary Bell, Michael Bradley (Chair), Dianne Davis
uty Chair), Lisa Lewin (Treasurer), Simon Burke, Tina Bursill,
Marchand, Kate O'Brien, Stuart Thomas

stic Director Nick Marchand
eral Manager Nathan Bennett
ninistrator Belinda Kelly
nce Manager James Wu

Philanthropy Manager Simonne Brill
Literary Manager Christopher Hurrell
Production Manager Miles Thomas
Front-of-House Manager Matthew Lilley
Front-of-House Supervisors Tim Derricourt & Nick Terrell
Publicist Lara Raymond
Graphic Designer Jeremy Saunders
Web Designer Julian Oppen (Full Cream Media)
Education Consultant Elizabeth Surbey

Griffin Donors

me from Griffin activities covers less than 50% of Griffin's operating costs – leaving an ever increasing gap for us to
hrough government funding, sponsorship and philanthropy. Your support helps us bridge the gap, keep ticket prices
rdable and our programs working at their best. To make a donation contact Griffin on 9332 1052 or donate online on
Griffin website www.griffintheatre.com.au

ARDIAN ($10,000+)
ymous x 2
ate Lady Nancy Fairfax OBE
Petre Foundation

.D ($5000 - $9999)
elStudio Pty Limited
ents Court Hotel

VER ($2500 - $4999)
ard Cottrell
n Jackman & Deborra-Lee
ess
f & Wendy Simpson
ph Skrzynski AM & Ros Horin

ONZE ($1000 - $2499)
ymous
der
orah Balderstone
d & Anne Bennett
ael Bradley
ael Choong & Harold Melnick
r Graves
Grumley Family
r Keel
ifer Ledgar & Bob Lim
h Longes
s & Fran Roberts
Late Dr Rodney F. Seaborn
OBE

SOCIATE ($500 - $999)
inette Albert
ppleton
gowan Films
Marchand

Parsons Family Trust
Rod Phillips
Mrs Betty J Raghavan
Rebel Studio Pty Ltd
Annabel Ritchie
Kim Williams AM

FRIEND ($100 - $499)
Steven Alward & Mark Wakely
Carl Andrew
Anonymous x 3
Gregory Ashton
Rob Brookman & Verity Laughton
Denise and Neil Buchanan
Simon Burke
Wendy Buswell
Terence Clarke
Victor Cohen
John Crocker
D.W. Knox & Partners
Di Davis
Victoria Doidge
Jo Dyer
Rosalind Fischl
Nicky Gluyas
HLA Management Pty Ltd
Janet Heffernan
Mary & John Holt
Beverley Johnson
Gloria Jones
Geoffrey Lack
David Lieberman
Ian Marsh
Neville Mitchell
Kate O'Brien
Brian & Lyn Oliver
Betty Raghavan

Anjali & Talitha Roberts
Arahni Sont
Ross Steele AM
Gary Sullivan
Roz Tarszisz
John Thacker
David Thomson
Robyn Tooth
Irma Trnka
Julie Wyer
Vera Zukerman

CONTRIBUTOR (<$100)
Robyn Ayres
Gary Balzola
Bronwen Bassett
Jane Bridge
Jason Catlett
Sharan Daly
Catherine Duggan
Gemma Edgar
Mrs R Espie
Elizabeth Evatt
Michael Eyers
Colin Fainberg
Belinda Firmstone
William Franken
Emily Hale
Noelene Hall
Norman Hams
Belinda Hazelton
Kevin Hewitt
Gary Hodson
Marianne Hoeg
Barbara Holmes
Joan Humphreys
Peter Ikin

Hazel Kelly
Mary Lawson
Stephanie Lawson
Caroline Le Plastrier
Jean Prouvaire
Christine Lozano
Sacha Macansh
Ruth Marshall
Andrew McMillan
Frances Milat
Tom Milligan
Peter Noble
Callan O'Neill
Doreen Payne
Dianne Pearson
Fiona Press
Ann Proudfoot
Jean Prouvaire
Bill Roberts
Warren Riolo
Catherine Rothery
Kay Ryan
Sharon Shapiro
Nancy Squires
Dr Leigh Sutherland
Helen Thompson
Beris Tomkins
Mark and Lynn Trainor
Douglas Trengrove
Irma Trnka
Jennifer Turnbull
Daniel Vucetich
David Wallace
Elizabeth Webb
Anna Zysk

2008 Griffin Partners

Principal Sponsor
PKF
Chartered Accountants
& Business Advisers

Venture Partner
gadens
lawyers

Production Partner
holding
redlich

Company Partners
blakehurst technology
CURRENCY PRESS
The performing arts publisher
www.currency.com.au
THE FEAROCIOUS FEED
FOXTEL
See something. Feel something.
fullcream media
REGENTS COURT HOTEL
SEABORN BROUGHTON & WALFORD FOUNDATION
SIGNWAVE NEWTOWN
TYRRELL'S WINES
UNSW
V & R THE VICTORIA ROOM

Artistic Partners
ARTS ON TOUR NSW
apa arts projects AUSTRALIA
HotHouse THEATRE
nowyesnow
Performing Lines
Riverside
tasmanian Theatre Co.

Media Partner
Time Out Sydney

Philanthropic Partners
COPYRIGHT AGENCY LIMITED
EQUITY TRUSTEES FOUNDATION
THE MALCOLM ROBERTSON FOUNDATION

Honorary Auditors
Rosenfeld, Kant & Co.

SBW Stables Theatre Owned By
SBW Foundation

Government Partners
Australian Government
Australia Council
arts nsw
CITY OF SYDNEY
Australian Government Playing Australia

Griffin is grateful to the UNSW School of English Media and Performing Arts for its ongoing rehearsal support.

Griffin Theatre is assisted by the Australian Government through the Australia Council, its arts funding and advisory body; and the NSW Government through Arts NSW.

Griffin acknowledges the generosity of the Seaborn Broughton and Walford Foundation in allowing it, since 1986, the use of the SBW Stables Theatre rent free, less outgoings.

OTTO RISTORANTE

"Vive Bene Mangia Bene"
"To live well is to eat well"

With a spectacular waterside location, great service and simple fine food, Otto Ristorante remains one of Sydney's most enjoyable and popular restaurants. Located on the Finger Wharf at Woolloomooloo, chef James Kidman describes his food as "...an expression of where and how we live; the flavour of the ocean, our paddocks and our gardens."

Great function spaces, ranging from an outdoor terrazzo to a private dining room in a 100 year old wool lift, allow the Otto team to create special dining experiences for groups ranging from 8 to 150 people.

Otto Ristorante is a proud supporter of the Griffin Ambassador Program.

Area 8 · 6 Cowper Wharf Road Woolloomooloo NSW
Phone 02 9368 7488   www.otto.net.au

www.ingramcontent.com/pod-product-compliance
Lightning Source LLC
Chambersburg PA
CBHW041934090426
42744CB00017B/2050